The Unpopular Truth

"If I speak The Unpopular Truth,
does that make me a liar?"

by...............

K i r k   N u g e n t

"The People's Poet"

To Elisa
Thanks for supporting
my Dreams...
Enjoy

Published by

Ironic World

&

SunRASon Production Company

WWW.SUNRASON.COM

New York * London

Published by
Ironic World & SunRASon Prod. Co.

Ironic World Co.	**Sun-RA-Son Prod, Co.**
P.O. Box 46	P.O. Box 2020
Bloomfield, N.J 07003	New York, NY 10013
Ph: 973-207-7897	Ph: 917-281-7449
email: ironicworld@aol.com	**email: sunrason@sunrason.com**
www.ironicworld.com	**www.sunrason.com**

Copyright 2000 Kirk Nugent
Design and layout by Tehut-Nine
Cover Design by Tehut-Nine
Cover Art by Shelli "Skillz" Gillis

Library of Congress Catalog Card Number: **00-090631**
ISBN: **0-9700793-0-3**

Published 2001.

Printed in the United States of America

Dedication

This book is dedicated to my son, JuVon Kirkland Nugent. The person who gave me love unconditionally and taught me how to do the same. While others loved me, *Just Because*, you loved me, *In Spite Of*. Chase your dreams baby sometimes they're all we've got, and more times than not, they're the only thing in this world that will ever be true to you. Always remember if you don't have what you want, you're not committed to it one hundred percent. You will lose many false friends while chasing your dreams, but the ones you gain in the process will be with you for life.

Acknowledgements

I want to express my gratitude to the Creator, thanks for the gift of words. To all who have supported my dreams and my goals, my love for you will follow me into the next life and beyond. To **Tehut-Nine** and Sun Ra Son Production Company for helping me get this work to you in a timely manner. To **Skillz** for the cover art. Special thanks to **Kayo** for believing, **Steve Donaldson** for introducing and encouraging me to slam at the Nuyorican, and to **Keith Roach** for giving me an opportunity. To **Tanya Keyes** thanks for all we've been through, and to **Tammy Carr** for always having a brotha's back.

Special thanks to everyone who supported me and helped to make this book a reality.

INTRODUCTION

This work is titled, **The Unpopular Truth**. I've found that human beings have a most difficult time digesting the *truth*. Americans especially cannot deal with truth when it comes to the issues of race and racism. The case of Jimmy "The Greek" is an ideal example. He said, "Blacks were bred to be bigger and stronger with a greater sense of endurance." Because of that statement he was relieved of his position from a popular radio station. When in fact what Jimmy spoke was the *truth* as *unpopular* as it was. The fact still remains that the biggest Black slaves were bred with the strongest Black slaves. We were bred like cattle for profit. However Jimmy was ostracized and called a racist for speaking **The Unpopular Truth**. Why, in a so-called Democratic society, a grown man is forced to bite his tongue is beyond me.

My goal with this book is to teach what I know to those who are unaware, so they might be able to rise above the perpetual mental enslavement that has plagued us for far too long. The *truth* doesn't always sit well with everyone, especially those who have systematically and habitually distorted and discounted the *truth*. They hide the *truth,* because they have always profited from keeping the masses in the dark.

When the *truth* does emerge, the forces of darkness shall rebel in the most violent, most devious, most diabolical manner one can imagine. Of course, the message that I'm sending via this book is *unpopular*, however it is the *truth*. It is contrary and in direct conflict with what these heathens have been spoon feeding us for centuries. Their initial reaction will be to attack the message and discredit the messenger, but regardless of how much you distort it, the *truth* can never be killed!

Kirk Nugent
"The People's Poet"

Table of Contents

The Unpopular Truth...

If I speak *The Unpopular Truth*, does that make me a liar?
Because truth burns like flames,
And hypocrites try to put it out like wildfire!
Now! What if I told you that devils conspired,
To give you a Bible that would require,
Your submission to the atrocities
That slave masters transpired?
And that blue eyed guy that you so devoutly admire,
HE IS NOT THE MESSIAH!
The cat in the pulpit that tells you he requires
Ten percent of your salary to save you from the hellfire,
He's an absolute liar!

Gain knowledge before you retire,
And you'll find that a secret order conspired,
To hide from you the knowledge that they've acquired...
So when I speak *The Unpopular Truth*,
You'll think that I'm a liar!
They tell you, you have to suffer like the saints
In order to gain salvation,
Then take your money and build this capitalistic nation!
Have you thinking that being broke is a blessing,
Because the real truth you've been missing,
So it's not your religion, but hypocrisy I'm dissin'
When I say, "Forget em and their Thanksgiving!"

Catholicism and Christianity were not given to you,
So that salvation you could win.
In fact, you've been worshiping a false doctrine!
False prophets gave you scriptures
Mixed with their pagan past.
You adopt it as your own, and the spell has been cast,
As they lead you through the gates of hell fast.
But if I speak *The Unpopular Truth*,
I become an iconoclast!
Dealers of deceit have you thinking
That for Jesus you're making all this fuss,
But show me in your Bible,
Where Jesus celebrated Christmas...
Good Friday and Easter,
All traditions to honor false pagan Gods,
From Egyptian Baal to Babylonian Nimrod.

In the Ten Commandments,
The Bible warns not to bow to anyone
But the Almighty,
Yet the Pope has millions bowing
To a statue he calls Mary.
No one reads to see the contradictions,
And that's scary!
Scared to challenge traditions,
Because pleasing a mortal man
Has become their desire,
But if I speak *The Unpopular Truth*,
Does that make me a liar?

Black People yell, "Black Power, Black Power"
As they pump the Black Fist.
But I see too little activist and too many hypocrites.
We need to sit down and shut our mouths,
Was it not Negroes who voted Dinkins out...
And Giuliani in?
Now they're begging this devil to repent for his sins.
It was Blacks that sold Nat Turner
And Denmark Vessey out!

Sometimes it was at gunpoint Harriet Tubman had to free
Slaves from the south.
Blacks executed Malcolm,
Because he was gaining too much clout!
Remember it was Blacks
That first captured Blacks on the coast of Africa,
Selling us into slavery to European scavengers.
Slave rebellion plots ended way before the attack,
Because most plots were sold out by Blacks!

Long before we knew the words to, "We Shall Overcome"
Blacks were the ones that sold out our freedom.
Sending tired Blacks to martyrdom.
Sellouts informed overseers
That field Negroes could become troublesome.
So now we march into the new millennium,
Not really free and still really dumb,
Failing to vote, while filling these prisons.
Negroes looking for a better life in heaven,
When they could lose their voting rights in 2007.
Failing to act as the situation becomes dire.
But if I speak the *Unpopular Truth*,
Does that make me a liar?

The media is the biggest proponent of racism on the scene,
In a fight, Tyson bit Holyfield, the media reported
That he was a savage being,
Dehumanized him, compared him to the beast Wolverine.
Few weeks later,
Two white kids killed thirteen.
Media reported that they were troubled teens.
They say, "It's not racism"
When White cops place our lives at stake,
But I never heard of a Black cop
Killing a White kid by mistake.
Black girls get raped
And murdered everyday with no airplay,
Almost three years later,
The media's still buggin about Jon Benet.

So don't tell me that against us the media didn't conspire,
But if I speak the *Unpopular Truth*,
Does that make me a liar?

Here's an *Unpopular Truth*
That would cause White supremacy to disappear,
Every time I attempt to speak it
They say, "Nigger don't you dare!"
Thomas Jefferson continually raped his slave
Sally Hemmings for over a period of years
But White historians labeled it a love affair!
Africans were civilized,
While Europeans were still living in fear!
Queen Victoria was called,
'The cleanest woman in England"
Because she took a bath twice per year!
Bathing was an intricate part of African Islamic religions,
While Europeans emptied their dung in the yard,
This was their tradition!
Even when on their menstrual cycle,
Bathing for Europeans were vague,
Remember it was their filthiness,
That brought about The Black Plague.
Kings relieved themselves in the hallways of castles,
This was the norm for European Empires,
But if I speak the *Unpopular Truth*,
Does that make me a liar?

Some prefer to stay blind to the truth,
So you might as well take the "Blue Pill"
And live in the matrix.
Let life bury you like a ton of bricks,
While you pray to your crucifix.
Devils politic,
To transfix
The six, six, six
In the mix!
While diabolical minds stay creeping
Jokers haven't figured out that they've been sleeping.

Binary codes got your weakness exposed.
Sitting in front of your 35' with satellite dish and cable box,
Thinking you are watching a program,
While you're being programmed and watched!
Believing E-Z Pass was installed
So your travels can be swift,
When it's only another tool for the feds to track you with.
ATM and credit cards locate you quick,
Email and Instant message
Let them know who you politic with.
Everything's in place so a Police State can benefit,
But I'm crazy when I say, "My spider sense is tingling"

They changed your Sabbath from the 7th day to "SUN" day,
He came and saw Indians, but you celebrate Columbus Day.
Remember our necks were broken on the gallows
To kill our hopes,
But fools don't know that ideas cannot be killed with ropes.
Twisting the truth to advance their greed.
But the biggest mistake they made
Was teaching me how to read!
Now things, that this poetic scene
Wouldn't contemplate or reckon,
I break down in four minutes and some seconds!
Not even your bullets can silence me,
Because even my son knows my poetry.
He wakes up to see against humanity devils did conspire,
So when I speak the *Unpopular Truth*,
He knows I'm no liar!

Programmed To Self-Destruct

Captain's Log: star date 2028
T minus ten and counting,
The Negroes in America are drowning.
They were conceived in greed,
And raised by hypocrisy,
Now the American Negro has met his destiny.
We distort their history,
Deprived and gave them pipe dreams to cherish.
We kill their dreams
Because where there is no vision the people perish.

T minus nine and counting,
We've programmed the Negroes to believe anything.
We tell them to be patient, the civil rights bill is near,
This keeps the wool over their eyes
As we advance them to the rear.
In the media, let us parade them as thugs,
Hoods and society's misfits,
Give them an inferior education,
Then tell them they have a mental deficit.

T minus eight and holding steady,
The genocide is just about ready.
Give them welfare as a means of complacency,
They'll never know
That the price of greatness is responsibility.

Let us place a burden on the male
Far more than he could endure,
Now systematically,
That will destroy the family structure.

T minus seven and all is well,
The CIA has now introduced drugs
In the communities which they dwell.
Have our officers slaughter
Their men in the early morning mist.
We'll use the jingle of money,
To kill the voice of justice!
If the Negro enters our communities,
Keep him off balance, make him a mental wreck,
Have our officers pull him over
For random spot checks.
Have them plant evidence and break the Negro's necks,
But in our community it is imperative
That our officers *Serve and Protect*

T minus six, now let the supreme race be cleansed.
We'll use unemployment
To rip away at the very fabric of their existence.
Give them a few token laws
Let them believe that these laws were God sent,
Deny them credit
And face them with perpetual disappointment.
Keep them discouraged,
Let them know at the end of the tunnel,
There is no light.
Control the media,
So liberal Whites will not be sympathetic
To the Negro's plight.

T minus five and we're almost done,
Refuse funding for schools,
But let us build more prisons.
HOUSTON WE HAVE A PROBLEM!

The Negroes are awaking,
Now they're saying that we are devilish.
We countered the attack by giving them
A White Jesus to cherish.
Assassinate the key Black leaders one at a time,
This will guarantee that the next set falls in line,
We determine which Negro they will support...
"LT. nominate Clarence Thomas
To the Supreme Court"

T minus four prepare to divide and conquer,
Impress upon the lighter Negro
That he is better than the darker.
Portray them as a people that are prone to violence,
Have them believe that their vote
Will never make a difference!
Shake their confidence,
Question their intelligence,
Exploit their innocence,
Destroy their influence,
Deny their excellence, plant evidence.
Attack form every angle,
And the Negro will have no defense!

T minus three and the Negroes
Are not in the least terror-struck,
They're oblivious to the fact
That they've been programmed to self-destruct!

T minus two and the hour is at hand,
To completely remove the Negro
From this promised land.
From the days of slavery,
His woman has always given him the courage
To endure even more.
Before we can destroy the Negro,
He must identify with his woman
As a trick or a whore.

Program him through his music,
As he laughs and dance,
He'll come to devalue his woman
Before he can awake from this trance.

T minus one, now let's try this on for size,
We have the Negro hypnotized,
Paralyzed,
Ostracized,
Supervised,
Disorganized,
Disenfranchised,
Institutionalized.
In short we have the Negro neutralized.
Now give him brand names
And watch him cosign his own demise.
Gather around gentlemen, we have a dead body to eulogize.
The Negro has neither political nor economic power,
The strong Black man
Has seen his final hour.
So on this chapter, let us close the door,
Gentlemen I'm proud to announce
That the threat of the American-Negro is no more.

Mars

You pollute the Earth with your political wars,
Now you have your satellite pointed at the stars,
With the hopes of exploring Mars
But just who do you think you are?

And what if you went to Mars and saw Martians
But they didn't speak your language?
Would you call them savages?
And rob them of their heritage?
Commit them to a life of bondage?
And use their bodies as experiment for Syphilis?
Would you give them facilities,
That were, *Separate but Equal*
And encourage them not to fuss?
Would you seat the Green Martians
At the back of the Martian bus?

Upon your arrival
Would the Martians realize their greatest fears?
Would you march them across Mars on a *Trail of Tears*?
Would you lynch the male Martians?
The ones you couldn't tame,
Whip the Green Martians and change their names?
Or would you exploit them just for the sake of greed?
Would it be a crime for a Martian
To teach another Martian to read?

Would you abuse them for generations,
You know, over a matter of time?
Would you make the color Green,
Synonymous with crime?

I know you would degrade them,
It doesn't take a genius to go figure,
You would probably start by saying,
"They look like little green niggas!"
Would you treat them as livestock,
And raise the male to become breeders?
Would you orchestrate,
The massacre of their Martian leaders?
And what if, there were a Martian King, and a Martian X
After you murder them,
Who would you slaughter next?
In the middle of the night
Would your Klansmen cut their throat?
Would they have to march for generations,
Just for the right to vote?
And when you write your history books,
What would be your version?
Would you see the Martians as three fifths of a person?
How many Martians would get a broken neck?
As your officers went out
To *Serve & Protect*

Forgive me,
But I'm just asking because I know what your
So-called explorations are worth.
Upon your arrival, you wiped cultures off the Earth!
So if you landed on Mars
The Martians would probably pray for death at birth,
So for the love of God

KEEP YOUR ASS ON EARTH!

40 Mill

Suckers spent 40 Mill to investigate Bill,
Because rumor has it he lays pipe at will,
From Arkansas to Capitol Hill
So suckers spent 40 Mill.
While across from the White House the homeless chill,
Junkies pop pills,
Senators shoot down civil rights bill
Cops violate us at will,
I mean shit is just ill,
But still,
Suckers spent 40 Mill
To see if Bill got skills.

40 Mill to see who Bill took in the sack,
'Cause rumor has it, he hit it from the back.
I heard he had two six pack and just went Black,
He was like, "Yo! Won't you let a President hit that?"
Now come over here and play on my sax
While I drop these sanctions on Iraq.
Forget about Abner Louima
And police crimes against Blacks.
Forget the difference in sentence
Between cocaine and crack.
Forget the poor in the trailer park shack,
And forget the nines, that these ten year olds now pack.
But let us spend 40 Mill to see who Bill took in the sack,
'Cause we need to know...did he hit it from the back?

40 Mill to see who's been making who moan,
40 Mill to see if Bill and Monica were ever alone,
And if they were, did Bill get blown?
What I'm asking is, "Did she play on his saxophone,
And make it grow into a trombone,
And if she did, did she speak into the microphone?"
40 Mill down the drain while the homeless moan,
40 Mill and you're sweating me
For a two grand student loan?
However you look at it, it's 40 Mill
We could've used to achieve new milestones.

40 Mill to investigate all these theories,
Ask Hillary, she'll tell you it's a conspiracy
To get her husband out the presidency.
And Bill said, "All these allegations I deny categorically"
In other words I never touched Monica Lewinsky,
Only Hillary handles the jimbroski
So stop pitting her against me,
Besides I've never been this popular
Since I apologized for slavery.
So forget Ken Starr and the playa hating Republican Party.

40 Mill, y'all must be insane,
Spending 40 Mill to defame slick Willie's name
Playa hating cause Bill got maaaaddd game!

40 Mill, now the story begins to unfold,
And Bill was like, "Damn! That fat chic told."
He called Betty Curry and was like,
"Sweetheart hurry,
Drop what you are doing and go see Monica forthwith,
And for God's sake recover all my gifts,
Cause she done broke the cup
From which me and Hillary sip,
And as far as Linda, umm!
Betty that chic is a TRIPP!"
CLICK!

He called Jesse Jackson
Because his situation seemed so unfair,
And said Rev. Jackson could you please say a prayer?
"It is obvious, yet a pity
But you should've never touched the titty.
Now even though you got caught
With your hand in the cookie jar,
Bill I just love that thing you did with the cigar."

Bill said, "Jesse Stop!
I can no longer concentrate, my head is spinning so fast,
The only thought that enters my head
Is that they gonna impeach my ass.
Kick me out of the White House flat on my back,
Why is this happening to me Jesse,
I'M NOT BLACK!"

40 Mill to keep you distracted,
Now they've got you tuning in like fools,
While you're watching Bill,
They're cutting funding for public schools.
40 Mill to keep you focused
On Bill and Hillary's marital problems
Now y'all tell me what that gotta do
With the price of bread in Harlem?
40 Mill to make you say "Yeah, he jerked her"
Keep you distracted
While GM lays off another two thousand workers.
40 Mill to make you watch
As Congress brings him to his knees,
Keep you focused on the bull
While they ship our jobs overseas.
40 Mill to make you say, "Hell yeah, Bill must pay."
Keep you blindfolded
While they execute Mumia in a few days.

It's 40 Mill hoping you'll be hypnotize
By their televised lies,
But I couldn't care less what Monica was doing
Between the Presidential thighs.
I'm not following all this litigation,
I don't care about Bill Clinton's frustration!
So don't let them distract you with their 40 Mill
And their stories about Bill
And his Oval office thrill,
And his DNA spill
Or any of the other bull that don't mean nil,
Because the ones who program, program with skill,
They instill in your mind what they will,
So chill.
Before you end up as one of these domicile imbecile,
That was programmed on Capitol Hill,
With 40 MILL!

Ironic isn't it

You swept us from our beaches,
And dumped us on your sands,
Black people in America
Were never welcomed on Ellis Island.
You changed our names to confuse our identity,
You deleted our religion and gave us Christianity.
You erased our contributions from your history text,
You change our thoughts, to one of divisiveness.
On your auction blocks you placed us up for sale,
Now you want to tell us about your angry White male?

We educated ourselves and now you see us as a threat,
Considering at one point teaching a Black person to read
Was a crime punishable by death.
Our schools are inferior,
While your kids are kept abreast,
Because you view educating Blacks as a conflict of interest!
You have no money for college grants
So we're denied our cap and gowns,
Yet you find forty-five thousand per year
To keep a Brother locked down!

You used religion trying to conceal your vanity,
Slaughter an entire race in the name of Christianity,
Manifest destiny was the Red man's enemy!
You displaced us as a nation when you stole us from Africa,
Now you want to tell us
About some bullshit contract with America?

You said physically, we're unattractive
And deserve to return to the dust,
Yet every year you die of skin cancer trying to look like us.
You argue that we're repulsive
And the Black man looks disfigured,
But Hollywood spends millions,
Trying to get her lips bigger.
You claim that we're inferior, your total opposite,
Yet you spend millions trying to look like us,
Sound like us,
Dress like us,
Dunk like us,
Ironic isn't it!

Now you claim that we're a burden to this country,
And the welfare system needs to be rehashed,
But for each Black on welfare, they're five White trash!
You condemn cruelty around the world
As you bring it to the media's attention,
But lynching first occurred in America,
It was an American invention.
You claim that we're lazy as a people,
One of God's worst creation,
But step back in time and you'll see,
It was the Black man that built this nation!

During slavery you lynched our men
And raped our women with a large mob,
A child lives what he learns, so yes America,
You taught us how to rape and rob!
You invented the rumor
That Black men lusted after White women
For most of their days,
When in fact it was the White master, who sexually
exploited his female slaves.

Historically, you stole from us,
Left us penniless and adrift,
Now at Christmas you want me to tell my son that some
White man comes down the chimney
And brings him free gifts?
What's Ironic is that Negroes fall for that bull!

Newt Gingrich shut the government down
Because for one flight
He was forced to sit at the back of the plane,
For years we were seated at the back of the bus,
And our cries went in vain.
We marched for equal rights,
You used fire hoses and treated us like filthy rags,
Now you want us to pledge allegiance to some revised
Confederate flag.

You kept us out of boxing
And the sport suffered a drought,
When we finally entered the ring
We knocked your punk ass out.
What about when we came out singing,
You claimed it to be nothing but crap,
Except of course for all the pieces that Elvis jacked,
Now a great percentage of your teens watch MTV
And buy gansta rap!

And if you think that's funny,
Umm!
Well, here's another paradox,
You claimed that our hair is nappy,
But you went and got dreadlocks!

You see, whatever we do,
You try and make a counterfeit,
Yet you despise us being Black,
IRONIC, ISNT IT?

Life Sentence

The crime I committed was unthinkable,
My attorney pleaded, "Insanity!"
He said that mentally I was unstable.
I stood before the court, adorned in prison rags I was filthy.
Has the jury reached a verdict?
"Yes, your honor, guilty
Let us give him life with no chance of parole."
But the judge said,
"No! That would destroy the body,
Let's destroy the soul!"

The minute he read the sentence,
My eternal torment began,
They dropped me in twenty-first century America
In the body of a Black man!
Now here I am a grown man
In a world that treats me like a child,
Wherever I went the cops harassed me
Saying that I fit some criminal's profile.
I try to walk the straight and narrow
But everyone treats me like a crook.
I tried to cross the street
And some old lady clutched her pocket book,
Gave me that look, as if I'm the one
That went across this country and
Everything the Indians had I took!
In the malls security follow me
Cab drivers, up front they wanted the fee.
On interviews they file my application,
Can't get a loan for my education.
In crimes I'm first in the line up,
To go to college, the Army insists that I sign up.

My civil rights they violate,
They left me despondent and desperate.
They say I'm militant when I try to resist,
As they used my body as an experiment for syphilis.
Gave me inferior schools and inferior housing,
Their banks engage in redlining.
I can now sit in the front of the bus,
Yet I remain at the back of the line,
The color of my skin is synonymous with crime.
Kangaroo courts just waiting to trade my life for time.

Their officers pull me over for random spot checks,
Formulate chokeholds to break my neck.
I was unarmed when their police gunned me down
In my town, with 41 shots,
Took the case to their courts and their justice system said
They saw nothing wrong with that!
In other words, Nigger how dare you seek justice
Knowing you're Black!
Damn near 200 years and I'm still fighting for freedom,
Sitting in police precincts pulling plungers out my rectum,
Swallowing tears, watching the law murder my sons,
On my person, planting cocaine and guns.
Singing that good ole boys anthem,
"Run nigger run!"

America watched as racists cops beat Rodney King,
Bringing him to deaths door within a degree,
Now you asking me, to trust a justice system
That came back with a verdict of not guilty?
"He wouldn't stay down,"
And Amadou Diallo wouldn't go down,
America has always felt threatened
When the Black man refuse to go down!
But I am here to stand in defiance of your racist alliance.
If this country was founded on a Christian legacy,
Then give me my place in hell,
Where we can all burn EQUALLY!

The soil of this land speaks for me, screams for me!
My tears and my blood dug deep in your soils
And the injustice it pondered.
Copulated with tormented souls of the Red man,
It changed the genetic makeup of your land.
Came back with a vindictive answer
Now, the very food you grow
Will eventually give you cancer.

My mere existence is a sin,
Every criminal has become my identical twin,
I'm an outcast like Rumpelstiltskin.
Lower than a snake in the grass,
Except I can't shed this Black skin.
Surrounded by hypocrites saying they're born again,
As they lynch me time and time again.
But I'm tired of being hung by ropes on oaks,
At the hands of the good ole Christian folks,
Sick of being the butt of their corporate jokes
As they sip on Diet Coke,
Puffing cigar smoke.
Act like they making us some concessions,
But their sins don't get mentioned in their confessions!
I live between a state of fear and depression,
Until I became Black
I never understood the psychology of oppression.
So how dare you try to act
As if all this injustice is in my mind,
When in my Black skin you've done no time!

I Believe

I never believed in the tooth fairy,
Hardy boys or Nancy Drew mysteries,
I never believed in the Bogeyman,
December 25, Santa Claus was not involved in my plans.
I had no faith in the Genie in the bottle,
And sometimes I question the validity of the gospel.
And being that I'm living in America,
My lucky diamond pinky horseshoe ring,
Couldn't cover the sins of my skin.
So in short, I don't believe in a lot of things,
And I damn sure don't subscribe to the hypocrisy,
But follow me when I say I believe in poetry,
Persistence, passion.
I believe in tailoring my life in my very own fashion.
I don't believe in accepting the leaves or the fruits,
Instead I want to dig up the tree and examine the roots.
But I do believe in my right to command this stage
And spit, *The Unpopular Truth!*

I believe that nothing in this world can ever deter me,
I believe that one man with courage is a majority.
I believe in letting the cat out of the bag,
Spilling the beans,
Kicking the real deal Holyfield.
So don't invite me to the mic
If you don't want me to keep it real.
I get raised eyebrows from conservatives,
When I say that the founding fathers were hypocrites,
And Thomas Jefferson was a rapist.

They look at me as if what I'm saying
Is some hidden mystery,
But don't hate me, hate your history.
As a matter of fact I'll say it again,
They were straight up hypocrites,
"All men are created equal" but I'm 3/5?
Good ole' massa Jefferson, a predator in the midst,
Congressman, Statesman, rapist!

They've been lying to you from the cradle to the grave,
When have you ever heard of a slave master
Having a *love affair* with a slave?
How you gonna accept the fallacy that they gave?
Do you not understand the definition of the word *slave*?
It means she could not oppose any advances that he made,
It means that she could not deny any orders that he gave!
It means she had no choice in the matter,
It means if she resisted her eyes would grow blacker,
As he back slap her, attack her, whiplash and unwrap her!
Talk to me like I'm grown and stop being rude,
Do you really think that at any point Sally Hemings
Could've said, "Massa Jefferson,
Tonight I just ain't in the mood!"
Please! He would've broke her down like a rubix cube,
Tossed her up like undigested food.
Get her acquainted with the heel of his boot.
With closed fist, split her lips and removed a tooth.
You know...the usual White supremacist foreplay
To get Black women in the mood!
Wrap her up like a Subway sandwich
He owned slaves, so we know the bastard was into bondage.
He probably would've took a pitch fork
To the back of her head
Like he was fending off some danger,
Kicked her legs apart and rode her like the Lone Ranger,
Smacked her around as he rearranged her,
Threaten to take her to the auction block and exchange her,
Brag to the other Senators about how he's gonna break her.
Probably cocked a shotgun in her mouth

So he could get off on her fear,
Rode her from behind as he uprooted her hair,
Call me pragmatic but that don't sound like a *love affair*

I don't believe that the human spirit can ever be outdone,
I don't believe NYPD thought Diallo had a gun.
I don't believe that with this racist Mayor
We'll get justice in the long run,
And obviously, I don't believe in biting my tongue.
However I question the hypocrisy
Of these voters who chime,
"How could God allow our kids
To be slaughtered in Columbine?
Where was He, isn't this His Universe
And doesn't He rule?"
But when will they learn,
This is America and God isn't allowed in schools!
So there, deal with that unpopular fact,
Maybe that's why no one got shot in the parking lot!
"How about that Mr. Fung?"
I believe America has a vested interest
In giving my son a gun,
I believe they're making billions
From pouring nicotine in his lungs.
No longer from trees,
But from legislative branches we're being hung.
I believe the racial divide has only just begun,
Because if they can keep everyone focused
On the bitterness of the past,
You'll be distracted long enough
For them to eradicate the middle class.
And when you wake up, it will only be the super rich
And your racist broke ass!

I believe in our ability to succeed,
And I believe in my right to make this pen bleed!
I believe in living on my terms,
Not living so that mommy and daddy can be fulfilled.
I believe in poetry, passion and the power of the will.

I believe that persistence is far more important than skills
But I damn sure don't believe in no diet pills.
I don't believe that women
Should fit in some prime time mold.
Given to them by some fat ugly beer belly media mogul.
Some cigar puffing, hair loosing middle age joker,
Some mediocre, chain smoker, porn broker!
Naw, I believe that women should be thick.
With thick thighs and thick hips
And a curvaceous bodacious behind
That makes my neck snap every time they walk.
After all meat is for the man, bones is for the dogs.

I don't believe in taking myself too seriously,
I've learned to laugh at Life's jokes,
I believe that J-O-B be an acronym
For *Journey Of the Broke!*
I believe that if you're unhappy on a job, you should quit,
But first call out sick,
Use all your sick days and vacation time fast,
Then tell the boss,
"You can kiss my narrow,
Black, Jamaican stretch mark covered azz"

I believe in being frank, I believe in being candid.
I believe that if you have something to say
Then get it off your chest dude!
I believe that you get ulcers not from what you eat
But from what's eating you.
I believe that nothing in this world is worth stressing me,
I believe that a woman brings out the best in me.
Ain't nothing in the world
Like a woman that turns me on mentally,
A friendship that grows to love eventually.
I believe that's just God's way of blessing me.

I believe that character, not skin determines the man,
I believe that racism is a fear of what we don't understand.
I believe that most lawmakers are insecure racist jerks

I believe in equal pay for equal work.
I believe that it doesn't make sense
For every dollar a man earns a woman only gets 75 cents.
I believe that if a good woman is the backbone of every man
Then the least we can do for our mothers and daughters,
Is give them their god damn quarter!

I believe that we need to look
A little deeper below the surface,
Because Blacks and Whites
Share the same common interest.
We both desire love, to feel wanted and needed,
But it's in the interest of a few to keep us divided.
Give us a preoccupation with color,
While they rape healthcare, leave us both in the gutter.
Tax your shelter so don't trust them with your funds,
Bleed social security and control the guns.
If it wasn't for George W,
These S and L scandals wouldn't be there to trouble you!
Strip you of your dough as they rape Medicare and HMO
But before you can focus and realize who's the real foe
They ask you,
"Aren't you sick of these complaining Negroes?"
Keep the divisiveness fresh in your head
While they have you on your financial death bed.

I believe the media's job is to manipulate, not to inform,
I believe that white sheets have been replaced
With blue uniforms,
I believe nooses have been replaced with nines
And like Bryonn said,
"Ignorance rocks dreadlocks sometimes."
I believe in Karma,
I believe that you will repay the debts of your sin,
I believe that the man who won't stand convicted
In his beliefs will fall for anything.
I don't believe in their illusion of inclusion,
Instead I believe in the science of noncompliance,
Defiance, self-reliance and strategic alliance.

Obviously, I believe in a lot of things,
But most of all, I believe in the power within.
I believe in poetry, persistence and living life with passion.
Chase your dreams!
Fear always buckle in the presence of action.
I believe that we're the cause of our own unhappiness,
I believe there's so much in us that we haven't tapped yet!
I believe in experiencing life through every single breath.
I believe that there is greatness in each and every one of you
And I challenge you not to settle for anything less!

9-2-5

He got up early this morning,
Hugged his child and kissed his wife,
There's bills to be paid, so he's off to his nine to five.
His goals aren't written,
To please his boss is his major scheme,
Trading his time for money chasing
That elusive American dream.
He hates the job, but has no one
In whom he can confide.
That whenever he punches that time clock,
He's committing spiritual suicide.
Dying inside, crying inside.
Looking at his boss, murmuring,
"God, I wish somebody would just shoot ya"
Not knowing that he's the god,
Molding this cancerous future.

He doesn't want to think about it,
But his fate is sealed,
Thirty-five with a thirty year mortgage,
And he thought it was a steal,
For real!
If he gets laid off, my God, how will he manage?
He's got a child in kindergarten,
One on the way and nothing for college!
Gotta keep up with the Jones'
So he upgrades his car,
His wife objects to the move
And it leaves emotional scars.
To be truthful,
She no longer makes love to him like she used to.
Them moans no longer seem home grown,
As she disconnects the caller ID,
Went out and got a personal cellular phone.

But no time to focus on that,
Gotta hustle the insurance and car loan,
He grabs his briefcase, kissed her on the cheekbone
And hurried back to the war zone.

"Hey Bob"
Fronting like he's fulfilled in that dead end job.
The boss threatens his security,
Demanding more production for his time.
"Yes sir, very well sir"
Frustrated and emotionally castrated,
He comes home and treats his wife like a swine.
He now works longer hours,
So in bed he's a sexual bore,
But he keeps pressing on,
Because at sixty-five he wants to be socially secured.
Living paycheck to paycheck,
Financially, he's one big mess.
He tried to refinance his home
Only to find that for the past five years,
He's been paying only interest!
No doubt, he's stressed,
Low on dough and just got taxed by his HMO.
You don't know?
Realizing that nine to five ain't no joke,
And J-O-B be an acronym for *Journey Of the Broke.*
He watches his dreams goes up in smoke,
Like a practical joke,
But gotta keep that mask on for the town folks.

Steady steppin and fetchin
Skinning and grinning,
Posing and posturing,
Shuckin and jivin
Poor clown barely surviving.
He's been working so hard,
And nothing, nothing has he gained,
He grabs a bottle of Scotch, trying to drown the pain.

Now he constantly fights with his wife,
And to him, she's no longer nice.
And he has this gut feeling
That the postman has been ringing twice.
Screaming, "Dear God why did you curse me?"
But as a man thinketh, so is he!
Not knowing that he's the god
That created this painful destiny.
This ugly reality.
Not schooled in the power of the subconscious,
The unseen controls the scene,
He died the minute, he lacked
The courage to live his dream.
You can never kill
That quiet whispering voice inside of you,
It will haunt you, taunt you
Pick out a wreath and casket for you.
He's a sheep, schooled in the art of following,
Now his soul's hollering,
He's got high blood pressure and an ulcer,
Not knowing that's how life punishes ya,
Damages ya,
When you refuse to live your dream.
Faith is the evidence of things not seeing,
I beseech you, step out on your dreams!
Now watch as life shatters this joker in the next scene.

He came home early, emotionally he was hot,
Found the mailman delivering to his wife's G spot,
Representing all the flavors of Hip Hop,
Have her heaving like she needed a cough drop
Didn't even know she was flexible like that.
Sucking chocolate syrup off the finger
That held her wedding ring,
He didn't even know that his wife
Owned a leopard skin G string.
The mailman turned his wife into a play station.
Working her like she was chained on a plantation,

Dropping strokes like he was chief of the Zulu nation
Like he was the good deacon and she needed saving.
Like he was Jesus delivering salvation,
Like she had a green card and he was Haitian,
Like she was hiring
And he was proving his qualification,
Like she was the rain forest
And he was planting vegetation,
Like he was a fiend and had not taken his medication!
And in her eyes you could see her appreciation,
She looked like a slave
That has just heard the emancipation proclamation,
And to massa she was showing her utmost gratification.

She had the candles and the hot wax,
Homeboy was still in his tube socks.
Had his wife legs pinned behind her neck,
Bouncing her like a rubber check.
He watched as the strong young buck,
Unhooked his wife like a tow truck,
Grabbed the back of her hair and instructs,
"Come on baby, blow on it for luck."

In divorce court, homeboy had a fit,
Alimony, child support, he lost anchor and ship!
The new car that he bought,
The mailman was whipping it.
His Scotch, the mailman sipping it,
His wife, no doubt, hitting it!
So later that night from the roof of his office
He took his life,
Because he discovered,
He could not capture the American dream,
Working Nine to Five.

Predator...................

I observed you from afar,
Even though I knew you were taken.
I heard your man throws a good dick,
And brings home the bacon.
But when I looked deeply,
I could see some emptiness in your eyes
That's when I knew I could step up,
And get my slice of the pie.
I knew in some particular area, your man had to be slippin'
If only I could find out where,
I could exploit it and make you start trippin'.
I knew my game had to be tight, my plan...legit!
'Else you could just hit me with that,
"See you in the next lifetime" bull.
So naaw, I stepped back and methodically planned my sh*t,
You're about to become the victim of a cold, calculated hit!

I proceeded to introduce myself
And explained how lucky your man must be
To have here on Earth, a girl of your heavenly beauty.
You smiled and looked away, well in fact you blushed.
That's when I knew I was making progress but,
"Hey, no need to rush."
I said, "Good-bye" and walked away confident
That the foundation was laid,
Knowing that it was only a matter of time
Before I would be getting paid!

The next day I saw you waiting for the bus,
And though I kept my composure, I was overcome by lust.
I told you I was going in your direction,
And offered you a ride.
You got in!
Now I'm one step closer to moving your man to the side.
We conversed a bit,
And I found in what area this brother had failed,
Though he may take care of business,
He doesn't pay attention to details.
He never seems to notice when you get your hair,
Your nails, your face done.
His mind is focused on business,
And he seldom has time for fun.
Though you're an angel, for you he never made a fuss,
So I stepped up to the plate and told you,
"Baby please, you're gorgeous!"

Starving for attention, of course you gave up the digits,
Now it was only a matter of time
To my will you would submit!
You gave up the numbers,
Saying we could only be friends,
Lovers...NEVER!
I thought how naive, "Yea baby, yea...whatever."

I said, "Sweetheart please, as gorgeous as you are,
I am honored just to know your name."
Hence, the beginning of the games!

Whenever you needed to talk,
I was there to hold your hand as we walked.
Whenever you cried,
I was there to dry your eyes.
Whenever you were down,
I built you a crown.
See, whenever we were together
I made sure the time spent was a blast.

I made you close your eyes
And put away all the horrors of the past.
I promised to take your troubles away,
As I placed a pedestal under your feet.
But the fact of the matter is,
I'm just a dealer of deceit!

Soon she came to see me
As one of the nicest men she's ever met,
And sure enough, I saw her as just some girl
I haven't slept with yet!
Yea...I knew she was caught in my emotional net,
But still she needed a few more lies...to get her wet.

So I compliment her on the clothes she would wear.
Paid attention whenever she did her hair.
Asked her about her day and her bullshit career.
Promised her silk and fine cashmere,
As I whispered sweet nothings in her ear.
I told her how she made my heart flutter
Whenever she drew near,
And to be without her is what I feared,
And no matter what happens I will always be there.
And, "God, if...if only you knew how much I cared"
And I told her a bunch of other bull
That women love to hear!

Needless to say, she saw me as a friend and her man the foe,
Took me in bed not knowing
She's being manipulated by a deceitful Scorpio.
And I remembered when she said,
That she wasn't with my plan.
That she had a man!
Even showed me the engagement band,
But still,
She fell for my program,
Of candle lights and slow jam
Now I'm reaching for the Trojans,
And she ain't even thinking about her man!

Your man just left and he's barely out the door,
Now you're calling, telling me
I made you cum like you never came before.
Not realizing that a simple test of life, you've just failed,
Now you're reaching for me, thinking you've exhaled!
You don't want me to leave, and you're begging me to stay,
But I'm a Predator baby,
And you weak girls straight up, my prey!

You had a good man, yes, he wasn't perfect,
Now here comes the Predator to exploit your weakness.
Whenever you have a good man,
Never focus on the small details he's lacking,
'Cause there's a Predator out there, somewhere, watching!
So even though you beg, we can't be together.
Baby I thought you knew
Besides, you cheated on your man,
Who's to say you won't cheat on me too?
I need a woman I can work with,
Not a superficial girl from around the way,
Who is gonna jump from bed to bed
Because of a compliment I forgot to pay.
So when you come with your soap opera story,
Wanting to be my bride,
All I gotta say is,

"SORRY HON, BUT THANKS FOR THE RIDE!"

Turned Tables

Dazed and confused,
Frustrated and fed up,
Numb by injustice,
Hopelessness won't even allow me to be pissed.
Tired of feeling like that one redneck in Montana,
Who keeps getting abducted by aliens,
Trying to explain his experience to a cynical nation.
No one understands my plight!
If only for one day I pray,
Not even to get back what they took,
I want just for a minute,
The shoe to be on the other foot.
Snatch America by her blonde hair
And shove her in front
Of a full length mirror, and scream,
"Look! For God's sake, look!"
Yes, if only for one day
I would love to place the shoe on the other foot.

Get four big Black bald brothers,
Give them nines and call them officers.
Then get one average White boy,
And to those racist cops, he's just another cracker.
Trailer trash suspect,
That they're there to keep in check!

Whatever happens I don't care,
Just make sure in the end
You've got me a dead White boy laying there!
41 shots later, your White son's lifeless body
Embraces the unforgiving ground,
And the four Black cops justify it by saying,
"He wouldn't go down."

Let me see the tears flow
From his mothers rosy pink cheeks.
Let me hear her in anguish, reflect on his dreams.
Let me see her broken spirit,
Contemplate how could her son die.
"He never bothered no body, why God, why?"
Show me her faith in America
When this country now changes the channel,
Turns a blind eye,
And Black politicians popping up all over saying,
"The shooting was justified!"
Let me see her lips trembling,
But still trying to console his younger sister,
Tears soaked the picture
She held of his Bar mitzvah.
Weak from disbelief,
Emotionally fatigued.
Fighting to believe in a just God,
Then have the Black racist mayor get on TV,
Telling her that the cops were only doing their job!
Let me see you contemplate that shit!
Give you an opportunity
To get acquainted with the term,
Sick and tired of being tired and sick!

For once let me see
That White mother bent over in pain,
Let me see her take him back to Sicily,
Israel or the Ukraine
And bury him in a pine box.

Let me indifferently watch,
As she fights back the knives
Slicing through her gut.
But have no choice than in a racist black justice
System to place her trust!
Watch as they move the trial to
Newark, New Jersey,
Pondering if God
Has lost his mercy.
Cynical Negroes snicker,
"It wasn't a crime, just a tragedy!"
Observe your White son's bullet riddled body.
Watching devils blame your innocent child
For getting himself killed.
This injustice makes you sick.
And after they screw you for the umpteenth time,
Listen to these callous Negroes
Saying, "Well, we agree with the verdict."

Let me see you live that shit day after day after day,
Then you'll understand
Why we ain't give a damn if the killer was OJ.
But obviously, you chose not to learn,
So I pray for the day, when the tables are turned.
Understand that I get no pleasure in
The innocent slaughter of a White youth,
But I'm sick of America acting
Like Ku Klux Kops just ain't the truth.
I don't want to see tears
Of hopelessness running down your cheeks,
Or your sons being slaughtered
Like hogs in the street.
But it seems like that's what it would take
For you to feel what I feel
So just for once America,
Admit that my pain is real!

When The Cops Murder Me...

When the cops murder me, who will fight for Justice?
Who will stand up and say, "Naaw man, stop this?"
Will you believe their story that I had two guns and a knife?
When you knew I was non-violent all my Life?
Will you believe the news report that I attacked the cops?
That's why they hit me up with nineteen shots.
Claiming that I stabbed the cop, yea, right through his vest,
When all them shots entered my back and exited my chest!
Will you investigate the evidence?
For the integrity that it lacked,
'Cause you know they murdered me
For **Breathing While Black!**

To them my life ain't nothing but a toy,
'Cause I never heard of Five-O
Emptying his clip in a White boy.
Saying it has nothing to do with race,
But them punk media be fake,
'Cause I have never heard of a Black cop
Killing a White kid by mistake.
We shout, "No Justice, No Peace"
But the death toll never cease,
They chill for a week,
Two weeks later police brutality increase,
They kill my mother, my father,
My brother, my sister, my uncle,
My nephew, my niece,
So I say, "Forget a march!"
I wanna read about some cops that's deceased!

I remember when "Peace"
Was the only word that came out my mouth,
After Diallo, I'm like, "The hell with it,
Kill em all and let God sort em out!"
Because the media acts like they're blind to my plight,
Like day after day with these racist cops
I don't have to fight.
The Police have never guaranteed
My safe passage through the night,
Because my Black skin seems to offend
Everything that's White!

I'm tired of waiting for my enemies to solve my problems,
I'm sick of seeking validation from them!
Four dead cops won't stop Mrs. Diallo from grieving,
Two wrong don't make a right,
But it damn sure makes us even.

So when the cops murder me, who will fight for Justice,
Who will stand up and say, "Naaw man stop this!"
How far would you go to get Justice,
What I'm asking is the truth,
See, I'm dead...what I'm a do with a lawsuit?
What I need is a dead cop laying right here next to me,
So I can kick him all through eternity.
So don't go marching just to get on TV
I'll deal with the Soul,
IF ONLY YOU BRING ME THE BODY!

Mirror Image

As I walked by the mirror I took a double glance,
Then I stopped and looked,
Thought to myself, "Umm deep!"
Because the brother in the reflection
Was damn near the epitome of everything
That I wanted to be.
Starred at the reflection and back tracked
To when my eyes were about in my knees,
And I remember when the reflection back then
Was just about the ugliest thing I'd ever seen.
I tried to step back in time
And put the pieces together consciously,
Which came first, the self-image or the reality?

I back tracked to before
I started reading Zig Ziglar and Dale Carnegie,
Back tracked to before Earl Nightingale nurtured me
Back tracked to before Les Brown tapes uplifted me.
Back tracked to before
Psychology books meant anything to me.
Back tracked to when I thought the Kybalion
And its Universal laws were fallacy.
Back tracked to before
I thought Deepak Chopra was deep.
To when the only thing my heart did was bleed.
When mentally I was weak,
When spiritually I was in need, indeed I was asleep.
I back tracked to before I adopted the philosophy,
"I will persist until I succeed!"
I back tracked to before I realized that I am a lion
And I refuse to walk with the sheep!
Back tracked to before I realized
That the slaughter house of failure is not my destiny,
Back tracked to before I dared life to run come test me!

Back tracked to before
I started molding the future with my present thoughts,
Back tracked to when indeed,
The People's Poet was damn sure lost!
I back tracked to when hypocrites thought
I was unworthy,
Back tracked to when their self-image
Was what I held of me,
Back tracked to when low self esteem imprisoned me.
Back tracked to when that kid in the mirror was ugly!

Stop the clock!
Took time out from all that back track,
Hope I didn't lose you,
Fast forward and came back to the future.
Pulled out and old photo album
From my childhood days,
And asked myself, "What gives?"
Because nothing has changed.
Yea I've grown a few feet,
But my head was just as big,
And I was always a scrawny little kid.
All of a sudden, I'm proud of me?
So I ask, "Which came first,
The self image or the reality?
The truth or the fallacy?"

I took it a little deeper,
Went inside my thoughts and prayed
For the opening of my eyes.
The Word returned to me,
"Kirk, wisdom will be given to the wise."
Because by now I've had it with their lies,
Their conspiracies, their spies
Planting the seed for our demise
But there will be no revolution
As long as we stayed glued to White lies
That are being televised.
The Word returned and instructed,

"You are here to change lives!"
Stop playing around,
Stop being a clown
Pay attention, don't get knocked out in the first round.
Look at your skin is it not Brown?
So why do you call it Black?
Or better yet, why do *they* call it Black?
And why do *you* accept that?
Son, that's where you failed the very first test,
Because in their language Black is bad
And words eventually manifest!
Remember, "In the beginning the word was made flesh."
The negative image
That society holds of the Black race
The mental plane must force to manifest.
Yes! Look at the language,
The fork tongue in which they speak,
It certainly doesn't uplift you,
As a matter of fact,
It keeps you meek as they trample you under their feet!
No longer the obvious,
But in subtleties you're being attacked,
Why is Angel's food cake White
And Devil's food cake Black?
Blackmail is a felony,
And melanin creates *Black males*
In a society whose goal is to make them felons.
Corrupt White politicians
Now complain that they suffer
From a, *Political Black Eye*
Which incidentally they received
After telling too many *"White lies"*
Dare to go against the grain and they label you a,
Black Sheep who eventually gets *Black Balled*
And *Black Listed*,
That's ostracized just in case you missed it
But done to a White person he's eccentric.
When mere filthiness almost wipe out all
Of Europe back in the middle age,

The only appropriate name
They could find was The *Black Plague*.
Maybe I'm searching too deep,
Because I'm seeing a million
Ways in which we're being lured,
I even detest the way the
White chalk walks all over the *Black Board*.

There is death and destruction in their language,
Fortunately hip hop came and somewhat changed it.
Infusing with life an infirm hood.
Run DMC yelling,
"Not bad meaning bad but bad meaning good."
Took Ebonics and exorcised the curse,
Hip Hop became the disenfranchised night nurse
As skilled lyricists moved the language in reverse.
Bad became good, and we were viewed as D-O-G-S
Now we're G-O-D-S.
Yes! Stress had us stressing in the hood
Hip Hop came, made stressing a blessing
And everything was, "All good"
But even in the subtleties of language,
Be it Ebonics or formality
It was the self-image that came before the reality.

Now back to me
Or should I say back to we
Because I'm merely a reflection of you
And you a reflection of me.
Can't believe that in the 21st century
Man's mind remain so hollow
That we still have racists
Campaigning against their shadows.
Not understanding that whatever
We bring into our lives
Is a reflection of what we are internally,
Our subconscious manifesting externally.
The woman in my life is a mere reflection of
Everything that's beautiful within me.

My son a manifestation of everything pure within me,
And you, a manifestation of every life I needed to touch
Mentally, spiritually, physically!
You are my unwritten destiny.

Ulcers are manifestations of negative emotions
That we need to get out of our system.
And the *Unpopular Truth* states,
"There are only volunteers, no such thing as victims!"
The self-image creates the reality
So even if it's fallacy,
Let it not label you "Inoperable"
It's best to fool yourself into believing
You're unstoppable!
Let the fools find it amusing
But I'm incapable of losing.
My mind be my girl and I'm careful what I feed her,
I watch my thoughts
Like J. Edgar watches Black leaders.
Thoughts create reality,
So self-defeating ideology get fixed quick,
I refuse to have my destiny played out in the matrix.
Neither moody nor menstrual
So I don't go with the flow
My words be uncompromised just so you know!

I refuse to harbor ill will
I refuse to be bitter
I have no internalized anger
To eventually grow into cancer.
Naw, I keep a smile on my face
And the world reacts to my charm.
Warning bells goes off
At negative emotions like alarms.
Because if there's no enemy within,
The enemy outside can do us no harm!
So no need to retreat, I can't be beat!

"Let's make man in our own image!"
Which means we are children of God,
His seed indeed.
Now if I'm a child of God,
A god is the only thing I can grow up to be.
An ear of corn cannot give birth to a mustard seed.
Get it? I can't be beat!

If this world be Goliath, then before you stands David,
And if it's only one soul,
K. Nuge gonna save it.
For I'm here to spark a flame, kindle the fire
Foster the spirit and straight up inspire.
I dare life to test me,
For my self-image is now forcing
The hands of destiny!
I'm unstoppable!
Ain't no mystery check my history.
I go by the name Oprah Winfrey,
Muhammad Ali or Mahatma Gandhi.
Paul Roberson or John Johnson,
A million different faces, that's me.
Berry Gordy, Bill Cosby they all be me.
Chain and cage me for 27 years in a cellar,
And I will rise to rule South Africa
Just call me Mandela.
My spirit cannot be broken by fear's stenches
I've been in these trenches for centuries.

I vividly recall when they said to me,
"Old man you must be blind,
You must've lost your goddamn mind.
Ain't nobody gonna spend any money to
Be entertained by a mouse or anything of that kind!"
Now Mickey Mouse is worth more than
Everyone in this room...combined!
I'm the spirit of Walt Disney.
Ray Kroc lives within me
I'm the true meaning of Manifest Destiny!

I cannot be deterred!
My vision be clear like that of Alexander Graham Bell,
When he invented the telephone
President Rutherford Hayes said,
"That's an amazing invention but
Who would ever want to use one of them?"
I'm guided by internal radar
Like birds on their way down south,
In 1962 Decca Record dismissed four young musicians
Told them, "Groups with guitars are on their way out!"
They left without a contract,
But refused to walk on pins and needles
Wasn't long after that, they released their first album,
And called themselves, "The Beatles."

Put down your fears and follow me,
Control your thoughts, go to your destiny.
But naw, you rather sit there and envy me,
Get on the internet and slander me.
But negativity serves to inspire me
Not to deter me.
So peace be unto you and your hostility!

With free will I control this sphere,
The God of this hemisphere
The devil cannot play here.
For I am unstoppable!
Impregnable, invincible, irreplaceable, indispensable,
Did I mention indestructible?
Unbreakable, unflinching,
Unyielding, unwavering, uncompromising!
That's right, I'm resolute.
Still a mere reflection of you.
I'm here because I've seen too many souls lost,
Too many people paying too high a cost.
Being too obsequious to the boss,
That's right...LOST!

What you are now experiencing
Is the sum total of your thoughts.
You've gotta change your thoughts,
Show some confidence
Cease from all that fretting,
Because if you keep on doing what you doing,
You gonna keep on getting what you getting!
"Ye are Gods and all of you
Are children of the Most High"
These words won't die, they certainly don't lie.
So why bow in the face of adversity and cry?
Faith will conquer fear and replenish your nerves,
"Choose ye this day which God ye shall serve."
As for me?
K. Nuge refuses to lose
Because you can either live your dreams
Or live your excuse!

They're Not My Heroes

They're not my friends, they're my foes,
I'm telling you now, these idiots are not my heroes.
And as sure as strawberries make me sick,
You could never get me to uplift
Or worship a baseball playing crack addict!
Not when my mother left Jamaica,
Came to America,
Worked for some racists as a domestic helper.
Four degrees below zero, in the dead of winter,
They had her outside grilling burgers.
All because for her three kids
She wanted to secure a better future.
So don't even think about forgiving me if I'm wrong,
Daryl Strawberry ain't did nothing compared to my mom.

We left Jamaica dead broke!
In high school I had two pairs of pants
And a used winter coat.
"Immigrants are taking all our good job,"
Middle America hissed.
"Go back on your banana boat"
Was the phrase of choice Negroes used when they dissed.
So for the longest, dad was unemployed
Mom, underemployed
And summertime in school
I was still rocking those two pairs of corduroy.
Found the American dream to be a hoax,
And for my clothing, the kids in school had mad jokes.
It was like Def Comedy Jam
When the class clown assembled his boys,

But I knew from Jamaica
That empty barrels made the most noise.
Here we had food stamp, name brand, welfare Negroes,
Turning their nose up, as if they were rich snobs.
I ignored it!
By fifteen I was reading investment books
By Charles Schwab,
And just like you saw on *In Living Color*, I had three jobs.
While kids in my class were unwrapping gifts
From under the Christmas tree,
I was reading, *How To Win Friends And Influence People*
By Dale Carnegie.
While cats blasted Eric B and Run DMC
I was listening to tapes of Earl Nightingale
Reinforcing, "Persistence is the key."
Doing paradigm shifts with my reality,
Fighting my insanity,
While simultaneously trying
To escape from what was obviously
A dysfunctional family.
Picked up a pen and found escape through my poetry.
Where the average sucker saw obstacles, I saw opportunity.
And by eighteen I'd decided that working forty hours
Building someone else's dream was not for me!

Took the road less traveled and found peace within,
While most of the thugs that I went to school with
Found lodging in the criminal system.
Telling me the White man made them victims.
And how much America is their enemy,
But idiots always
Confuse bad management with destiny.
Girls that lived to put broke immigrants down
For the entire school year,
I now see them with three kids,
No baby father and a part time job as a cashier.
While immigrants that I knew who slept five to a bed
Went on to become aeronautical engineers.
My goals are written precisely and clear,

Most are already accomplished, the rest are near.
And I can recall that it wasn't too long ago
When I stepped off
Air Jamaica with damn near zero,
So call me Bruce Wayne or Clark Kent,
Cause I'm my own goddamn hero!

Not Kobe Bryant or Wayne Gretski,
Eddie Murphy or Andrew Agassi
Funk Master Flex or DMX,
Sylvester Stallone or Toni Tony Tone,
Not one of those jokers get revered in my home.
To put shoes on my son's feet
I'm out here breaking my balls,
And you think I'm going to give the credit to some myth
You call Santa Claus,
Or some cross dresser that so happens to be able
To rebound a basketball?

No, my hero is the grandmother with arthritis,
Who crawled out of bed
Just to make her grandson a sandwich,
That's my hero, forgive me, I meant heroine
I'm talking about the woman
Who is not looking for a glass slipper,
Because she's too busy shattering glass ceilings!
Rosa Parks made her stand by sitting down,
Justice peeped through one eye
And tried to give me the run around.
Not knowing that Sharpton would turn
Jersey State Troopers insides out, upside down.

Forefathers risked being whipped to death
Trying to learn the difference between noun and pronoun,
Angelic Black wombs used
By capitalistic devils as breeding grounds.
I survived broken down, hand me down,
Scale down shantytowns
And even politics that were trickled down.

But instead you are asking me to idolize these clowns?
Well I'm here to give props to the single father,
Raising his daughter.
He's up way before dawn,
But gotta deal with her vindictive mom,
Who insist on using the child as a pawn.
I'm here to recognize the teenage girl,
Who got pregnant in High School not knowing,
How the hell she would manage,
But aborted the abortion, went on and finished college.
Instead you want to give me Lil' Kim,
Lewd and damn near nude,
Or some other idiot that can't recall
Where he left his dogs at,
That's the image you give to my son and say,
Go emulate that!
That is neither cute, classic nor phat!

The Hitler in Gracie Mansion says
He wants to now fingerprint welfare applicants
For the first time,
Giuliani has officially made poverty a crime.
In the Bronx, he had his cops murder me,
Move the trial to Albany,
Now four racists freed by an Uncle Tom jury.
Telling me the city has no money,
For the homeless as he turns the knife's blade,
Yet dropped millions of dollars
For a Yankee ticker tape parade.
Christmas he's with the Cardinal doing midnight mass,
But who's he trying to impress?
And why doesn't O'Connor protest,
Remind Giuliani that Jesus himself was homeless.
Here's a demon with no compassion, far removed from pity,
But he's supposed to be my hero
Because he curbed jay walking in still a racist city?

I forego their game show years ago,
Got sick like vertigo,
Stood tall and spit in the face of Jim Crow,
Because if nothing else, I know,
I came from a people who parted waters
And told Pharoah to let my people go!
A people who were robbed of everything that they sowed,
A people who were said to be illiterate,
But dominated the talk shows,
A people whose justice has been held in escrow,
A people who have been constantly delivered low blows,
But met adversity head on and responded with K.Os!

My heroes get no coverage in the media,
I ran off with three gold medals
When Hitler said I was inferior.
My heroes have clean hands and pure hearts,
Sat imprisoned for twenty-seven years,
Came out and tore a racist government apart.
My heroes stood up to guilty governments
With poisonous doctrines,
Hypocrites claiming that their agenda's bigger
Became vindictive when Ali asked,
"How you figure?
You gonna send me overseas
To pull this M16's trigger
When no Vietcong ever called me a nigger?"

So sorry you can't manipulate me
Into killing another man of color,
Under the guise of patriotism,
So I can return from Vietnam
Just to be subjected to your racism.
My heroes faced adversity on the daily,
They dreamt, "By any means necessary."
So you can keep that bull
You try to spoon feed on prime time every night,
Because if nothing else, history has taught me
What my heroes are supposed to look like!

Copout

Forget the sellout,
Tonight it's the copout, I wanna talk about,
The Negro that's quick to come out his mouth,
Yell and shout,
Puff and pout,
'Bout his financial drought,
Telling me the White man keeps watching his whereabouts.
The same Negro that has six kids down south,
And has yet to put bread in their mouth!

I'm sick of Negroes using their Blackness as a crutch,
Telling me the "White man" done did them such and such.
Saying that the Jews are robbing them blind,
And in their neighborhood, Korean stores are all they find.
Complaining that the Arabs are pimping us like whores,
But he just dropped half his check
In that Arab liquor store!
Saying we should make it so these damn Chinese starve,
Five minutes later he comes back
With four wings, fried hard!

I am not trying to hear about your conspiracy,
When you're high off that Henessy.
Coming back from your spending spree
In your chromed out Cherokee
With your ruff neck company
Bragging about your felony
Steady telling me
About your calamity,
And how the White Man is the cause of your every agony!

I am sick and tired,
Of Negroes living a life that's gonna cause them
To self-destruct,
Then copout by using their blackness as a crutch.
A lot of these Negroes, I'm not feeling them so much!

Copouts, quick to complain about the racist laws
That politicians wrote,
They complain all day,
But election night they won't even vote!
"The White man won't give me no job"
First words out their mouth,
Going on interviews, Ebonics out!
I know cats late for work every single day jack,
When they get fired,
"Man that would've never happen if I wasn't Black"
Ignorant Negroes quick to run to the mall,
And every dime they earned spent,
Knowing damn well they're two months
Behind on their rent!
Trying to justify it with that racist chat,
But can't explain to me exactly
How the White man makes you do that?
Tell me how he makes you spend all your money
At Christmas time,
So that until you get that rapid refund....
You don't have a dime!
Ignorant Negroes quick to spit that, "Yea man it's all good!"
But when life goes wrong,
They riot and tear up their own neighborhood!

I am not saying that racism doesn't exist,
But my skin has never been a crutch,
When Life goes wrong, I'm going to STAND UP!
I am not about to count myself out,
Yell and shout, puff and pout
Because, the Negro that does that
Knows not what he speaks about!

Look at my history,
Am I not the epitome of success?
I caused pyramids to manifest and left devils impressed!
Survived the stress, when my child they molest
Nevertheless, taught their kids how to love and caress.
Nurtured their suckling on my delicate breast.

I toppled Mt. Everest and rode their pony express.
Slaughtered monsters in the Loch Ness
So they could go west.
It was on my back that they built U.P.S!
Check the DNA of their success,
And you'll find my blood embedded in their progress!
Before my arrival, this country was a mess.
If it wasn't for my free labor,
There would be no Gettysburg address.
But that's one truth they won't profess on CBS,
Tune in to the news
When you're ready for the real B.S.
I stood on the front-line
Of their battlefield when they were in distress.
My neck was a rung on their ladder of success.
They raped my princess, and made her a mistress!
YES!
It was on my back that America built her success.
So when you talk endurance,
I AM THAT LITMUS TEST!
Forget what you heard
I'm here to testify inasmuch,
**THAT THIS BLACK SKIN
AIN'T NEVER BEEN NO CRUTCH!**

I No Longer Write About Depression

First I was afraid, no doubt... petrified!
Reflecting on my life
Wondering how I survived?
I recall my childhood,
Always wanting to runaway or commit suicide.
Always fearing having company,
Because that's when I would be stripped of my pride
Esteem tossed to the side
As parents transformed into Jekell and Hyde.
I recall being the best and the brightest in school
Winning a full scholarship, awards, mad stuff,
Only to come home and feel like you're not good enough.
I remember kneeling by my bed praying to God
For the end of my days,
Walking by the cemetery
Envying the lucky bastard in the grave.
I remember wanting out so badly...
That I wouldn't take my medicine for sickle cell,
Hoping I would have a crisis and it would just kill me.
I remember being unclothed and disrobed
And stripped down to my little white fruit of the loom brief
And being beaten till the blood broke freely from my skin.
And as a child, trouble was something I was never in.
My dad justified it by saying responsibility he was teaching.
He used all manner of electrical wires,
To insure that my eight year old skin stayed on fire.
By nine I concluded that parent's love
Was just too much for any child to desire,
And if you looked into my eyes, it was obvious,
They had successfully extinguished my fire!

But given a choice, if I had to choose
I would choose the beatings over the emotional abuse.
Even though I can recall being beaten
Till my spirit cried no more, laughed no more!
Loved no more.
Self worth packed up and walked!
Teachers would send for my parents, asking,
"What's wrong with Kirk,
He's so bright but he doesn't talk?"
Would you? After being beaten damn near half to death
Because you forgot to feed a dog?
To this day I can hear both parents voices reminding me
How much they regret bringing me into this world,
And back then I nurtured suicidal thoughts like
Steinbeck nurtured The Pearl.
Sickle cell had me laying in hospital beds
Pondering what's taking God so long to kill me,
My parents were good Christians
They deserved to be happy!
Sick of being stripped of my self-worth,
Robbed of my esteem.
Feeling like an expense waiting to be disposed of,
Always feeling unworthy of.
Felt no more needed than a pair of metal glove,
And I tried to mask the pain
By acting like I wasn't fiending for their love.
But who was I fooling?
I wanted it more than OJ wanted an alibi,
And in the process of trying to gain their acceptance
I inadvertently committed spiritual suicide.

But parents found new and improved ways
To batter and bruise me, humiliate and refuse me!
Mom did the church thing on Sundays,
Dad read the Bible damn near daily,
And I hated dogs and Christianity.
Lived in a world of illusions and hypocrisy,
By the time I discovered this poetry
Depression was in bed with me

Loneliness slept with me,
Unworthiness got dressed with me
The pen and paper fought to maintain my sanity
For my spirit had long abandoned me.

Low esteem was nothing new,
And eye contact was just something I didn't do.
God forbid I had to talk to you
I kept my eyes focused on my shoe!
Plastic smiles conveniently constructed
To mask internal rain,
And all I wrote about was depression and pain!
I was walking that thin line
Between being suicidal and homicidal,
Had a four five and a gloc nine,
And knew if someone pushed me
We would both loose our minds.
Because back then I wasn't trying to change my luck,
I was young, Black, armed and dangerous!
Thinking leaving this world in gun smoke
Would be glorious!
Back then me and my Jamaican clique
Was re-defining the term notorious,
We were ready to die
And these gang recruiters were adoring us.
But even the toughest gang member
Knew we were crazy Jamaicans
And they best not be provoking us!

Before you could say the words, "Racial profile"
I matured to that level
Where one starts becoming aware of racism.
Now my anger, frustration and hatred grew to another level,
Convinced that God was against me,
I was determined to team up with the devil.
I would watch nightly news reports
Of police brutality and it fueled my rage,
Wasn't long before me and the devil was on the same page.
I mean totally in sync

And my only goal before I die
Was to murder an entire precinct.
I went against the grain, fought against the norm
Masturbated to thoughts of putting holes in blue uniforms.
I was tired of sitting back watching the oppressors
Wrapping noose around the necks of the oppressed.
Tired being the victim, tired of being the oppressed,
Tired of being the helpless.
Wasn't looking for that Dr. King
"We shall overcome" type justice,
I was pissed, my guns were livid and the devil was like,
"Kirk we can do this!"

But God has a funny way of molding the future
Found out I was soon to be a father,
Decided that this lifestyle could go no further.
I remember being in the delivery room,
Looking in my son's eyes
Thinking I don't care what the psychologist,
The psychiatrist, the psychoanalyst writes,
This cycle of abuse dies tonight!
I vowed to him, "I will never shed your blood,
Nor intentionally bring a tear to your eye.
And you will know that you are loved
From the day you are born until the day you die!"
Gave him my name, which was a selfish thing to do
But just for once I wanted to hear a parent say the words,
"Kirk I love you!"
Who knew that it would take a baby to change my life?
Who knew that it would take a child
To change the way that I write?

Because I no longer write about depression,
Through my child I've found myself
I no longer write about depression
Because Kirk don't get depressed.
This world can't make me stress,
Perturbed, perplexed, anguished or distressed!
With the obstacles of this world

I'm neither moved nor impressed!
My God has found and delivered me from all my fears
Into a well of hope,
He's transformed those years of tears
Yes he was there,
When no one called, no one came, no one cared!
And if I had to do it all over again,
If He placed me in the fire, put my head to the gun,
I wouldn't change a single thing,
Because I love the person I've become!
My sprit can never be eaten by flesh,
The People's Poet is not the devil's conquest!
I've got a story to tell and through it
I've resurrected many souls from the dead,
If spiritually you're empty,
Then tell the world I've got bread!

I no longer write about depression
Instead I let my soul manifest, flew the cuckoo's nest
Took the litmus test,
I'm here to testify so can I get a witness?
I placed fear and doubt under cardiac arrest!
I pulled faith, hope and confidence from my war chest
Laid all insecurities to rest.
My spirit has returned, vowed never again to be oppressed!
I strapped on persistence as my life vest,
Now I'm heading north by north west
And I dare depression to run come test!
I've dropped the burden I've been carrying around for years,
Lift up my eyes unto the hills and declare
Regardless of what parents had to share,
I AM WORTHY OF BEING HERE!
My son has taught me how to love and how to live
Through grace I've risen,
And I have nothing but love to give.
My past is buried in the past
And from this day forth I shall live
I no longer write about depression
Because by God I've learned how to forgive!

She Was Everything To Me

It was on the eve of a previous life that we first met,
She foretold my trials and tribulations,
Promised she would return to walk me through
A thousand deaths.
Said I had to heal myself before I could heal the nation
Told me it was eons ago
When she first walked from the ocean floors
With time in her hand
Sat in the corner of a distance galaxy
Observing the vanity of man.
She said she traded the Gods,
Two pulsars, a nebula and a supernova,
So they would advance her to the future.
Just to warn me of my impending disaster,
She said, "Here take this it, will help you think clearer."

Now here we are present day,
And the pieces are finally coming together.
I searched her eyes wondering
Why it took me forever to embrace her.
Invest in her, my emotional currency
How could I have overlooked her beauty?
I must have been deaf,
Because I swore her eyes said that they loved me.
The scent of her body shackled my heart
And arrested my soul.
She declared that my story must be told!
Yes, she was pushy, raw, uncut, spoke from the gut.

If her heart felt it,
Then that was the lesson the tongue dished,
Women despised her, men labeled her a bitch.
One lesson she taught me way before I was twelve
Is that bitch was just an acronym
For *Babe In Total Control of Herself.*

At fifteen when I was bent on destroying the world,
Rebelling against what parents had taught me.
Realizing that Christianity was synonymous with hypocrisy,
This so-called Democracy was fuckery,
And Babylon live fi murda we!
The only public housing we build are the penitentiaries!
I live in a system that lives to divide and conquer,
Saying, "This doesn't concern you, it's about gay rights."
Or it's about women's rights,
Or civil rights or the right of the handicap
Knowing damn well it's about human rights.
So their plight is my plight,
Their fight, my fight!
I've met hypocrites claiming they serve a living God,
Damn near sixty-five and still haven't lived.
Saying they worship a loving God,
But have no love to give.
A God of peace, a God of mercy,
A forgiving God, a God of truth!
These same hypocrites hates fags, niggers,
Spics, kikes, chinks, gooks,
Never showed mercy to that homeless mother in the hood,
And as yet to forgive their parents
For their ungodly childhood.
It came to a point where I could no longer
Tell the difference between volunteer and victim,
I just wanted to take a dull knife
And gut this stupid system.

It was that night, she came to me,
Told me to close both my eyes in order to see.
She declared, "Boy, shut your mouth and speak!"

There were more mysteries in her eyes
Than the Bible and Koran combined,
Told me I was a vessel, but was given limited time,
She told me that, *The Unpopular Truth* will be difficult
For many to take,
Therefore I will judge you by the enemies that you make.
Keep your eyes close, and walk by faith,
Now tell me why fools find other fools to emulate?
Why does hate, so easily contaminate?
Tell me what makes the great, great?
And what causes gods to believe
They're nothing more than primates?

I said, "I see beautiful women trying to hide insecurities
Plastering on makeup all day.
But like all other false foundation, it washes away.
I see women failing to realize
That until you sleep with a man
All you've met is his representative,
An ambassador for his penis.
The diplomat who for the candle light dinners
He's willing to splurge,
Sleep with him once and the real dictator will emerge."
I speak for the forgotten soldier
Who bled to death in some cold,
Dark, damp, disgusting trench.
Died for his convictions regarding democracy,
Just to be buried in hypocrisy!
Same government he died for sold drugs to his family.
Reinvest the profits and built his son
A lifetime stay in a modern penitentiary.
I cry for the pawns in this game of chess!
Wanting to make a difference, but they limit our mobility,
Brainwash the entire faculty.
I see unseen hands pitting you against me
And me against you,
In boardrooms they collectively divide the two.
Telling you that my Black skull you should bash,
Telling me you're nothing but White trash.

We're both pawns in this New World Order,
Because even in your White skin
You're not allowed to cross their elitist border.

I see the devil's signature all over the dollar,
I see nations being deceived by Rhode scholars.
I see sheep walking down a path
That they have yet to investigate,
World Power being dictated by initiates.
Population control is the goal
As devils barter for your soul.
Slowly changing the morality,
Having you embracing homosexuality.
Can't you see they're tightening the noose?
Don't you get it?
Two men can never reproduce!
The puppeteers have you in a trance,
Have you killing your babies, returning to the dance.
Fine you with a slap on the wrist
So it's not even a deterrent,
Yes, I see disaster brewing in the undercurrents.

They reap the benefits while to some distant God you pray,
Notice how they change your Sabbath to Sunday.
She said, "Kirk you're preaching again,
History have burnt many preacher at the stake!"
My response was, "I speak the Unpopular Truth,
So judge me by the enemies that I make."
The truth that I speak, until the day I die.
Them words I will defend,
If a man refuse to live in peace,
Then he should rest in it then!

I see jokers trying to copy my style,
Not knowing that I drop my lines,
In encrypted rhymes,
Too subtle for the average mind.
So they run out and kill their dreams,
While I execute mine!

I looked in her eyes and the world became right,
Tasted her tongue and History stood corrected!
There was something in her kiss
That consumed me immediately,
She held court with my heart
And I wanted no mercy.
Her body, a tulip covered with midnight dew,
She inspired everything that I had ever hoped to do!
I buried myself in her love
And was resurrected a better man,
The thing that she gave me to think more clearly,
I held in my left hand!
Her flames engulfed my Soul,
Poured fire in my eyes and prepared me for this role.
I was drenched in her love,
Soaked in her sweetness,
Doused with desire,
Became pregnant with passion,
And gave birth to affection.
She was dinner by candlelight,
Sex by moonlight,
A spiritual delight,
The first date that stayed over night.
The reason why I stand before you, here tonight!
To true love she led the way,
She is the reason these eyes never strayed!
The one who restored my sanity,
In short she was my Poetry.

If Thinking About You...

If thinking about you were a crime,
Then convict me and take every dime.
Sentence me to maximum time,
Because woman, you stay on my mind!
Your ways how sweet, how tender,
Convict me now for I am a repeat offender.
Let not the Pope forgive me
Let the Governor condemn me,
Because the thought of you is embedded in my destiny!
Of your thought, I have a lifetime subscription,
Should it be canceled, then bring me the lethal injection,
For your love is my affliction,
Your lips, my addiction...
Your kindness I could never forget,
Your beauty cannot be offset
So let the high court sentence me to death
For I haven't begun to love you yet!

If thinking about you took away from my poetry,
Then let me write no more!
Let me be as eloquent as Mike Tyson on the Senate's floor.
Let mine be the novel that was never written,
For I am smitten!
There be none so majestic in all of Great Britain.
I want for nothing, for you are my all,
Your beauty be the reason cavemen chiseled on walls!
If spring could be personified, it would have your face,
If the angels came to Earth, they would envy your grace!

To be with you...
There is nothing that I wouldn't do.
I would switch from Methodist to Baptist,
From capitalist to Communist,
From spoken word artist to vocalist
From team slam to soloist,
Whatever it took, baby so be it!
Because one kiss of your lips,
And I'm in heavenly bliss
Everything gets dismissed and you become the emphasis.
My Revelations, my Genesis,
Woman, I fiend for this...
If I could no longer think of you, then let me not exist!

Extinguish my fire and send me into the great beyond,
If your touch no longer stimulates a response.
Let me rot in the jungles of the Amazon,
If our lips could no longer correspond.
Let the heavens realign the protons,
Neutrons and the electrons.
Let there be great destruction
From Pakistan to Oregon!
Let peace be gone
And there be great phenomenon
If your face I could no longer look upon.

Let my days be numbered and my death be a slow one,
Let me follow the destruction of the siren's song,
Let me break out in sores,
For which there are no cures...
If for another I should lust,
If I should betray your trust,
If for you I should no longer make a fuss,
Then condemn me to the planet of Romulus,
And my fate, have the Klingons discuss!
Hang me from my esophagus,
For chasing an inferior stimulus.
Leave me dangling and split me from the seam,
If I should gaze on anyone but my Black queen!

J Want To Write

Words transcend time,
They touch the souls
Of lives that haven't been conceived yet.
Our books will be read,
Our CDs will be played long after our deaths!
So what does it profit a man to gain the world
And lose his soul?
I've seen wisdom in the youth
And fools that were thirty years old.
I've seen poets prostitute their morals like
They were in a porno flick,
Racing to the stage just to suck their own dicks.
Egos get bruised and poets fly into a rage
As if it were the norm
On this stage I've seen low self-esteem
Manifest itself in at least twenty different forms.

I've seen poets come to the stage with no substance,
Nothing but dramatic hype
Trying to convince us that my God, and your God,
Hath commanded them to write!
I've seen poets wanting so badly to fit in,
Not being a part of "The big dawgs" is their greatest fear,
Grown men with kids, still falling victim
To pressures of their peers!
I've seen tens of thousands died innocently in Turkey,
I've sat back and watch the health care system do us dirty,
Over zealous cops waiting to serve me.

Politicians line up to jerk me.
I've seen souls die,
When all they needed was one encouraging word
To make them feel worthy.
Still I see poets coming to the stage
All puffed up like they're royalty.
Want the world to bow to them
Because they wrote some poetry!

I've seen poets names unintentionally left off a flyer,
And for weeks they remain vexed.
In this game I've seen big egos come
With even bigger inferiority complex.
I've seen poets run to the stage
And deliver nothing but low blows.
Small men enslaved by big egos,
Led astray by their amigos,
Idiots! Looking up to imbeciles as heroes!

I've seen poets been in this game for years,
And has yet to lift one soul higher,
But let them tell it, you'll swear to God
You've met the messiah!
Blockheads dripping with counter productiveness,
Feeblemindedness,
Idiotic, moronic and unconsciousness.
A literary reject, with a compromised intellect.
Joker come on stage, unprofound like that
But swear that egotistical crap was phat!
Never a kind word to leave their mouth,
Some poets be ugly from the inside out.
But I ignore them when they roll up week after week,
Because the more attention you give these idiots,
The more they seek!

I've seen poets write with only one goal,
And that is to pull down their neighbor.

Dying to be an icon,
Because someone taught them
How to mate a pen with a clean sheet of paper!
Like I've said, I've seen grown men with childish behavior!
I've seen poets glorify their gift to the whole nation,
As if self-praise is some kind of recommendation!
Hypocrites come on stages with masks,
Trying to deceive you and me,
Poor fools don't know that their wicked ways speaks
Volumes louder than their poetry.

And as sure as day will eventually turn to night
Poets will continue to turn knives in backs
And mics they'll jack,
For two seconds more under the spotlight.
Convinced that being an ass is their birthright.
Quick to talk about their third eye, yet they lack insight.
Running to the mic only to feed their egotistical appetite,
But what's the use of being a poet
If you're not gonna touch one soul tonight?
What's the use of being a poet
If you're going to make us regret
That we stayed to hear you on this open mic?
What's the use of being a poet
If you're not going to make a difference?
If your entire agenda is built on
Burning bridges and constructing fences?
If you only write to impress chicken-heads
And start beef that's senseless?
You need to chill with your material,
Revise it and spend more time,
Because that bull you come on stage with
Is nothing but the idiotic ranting of an inferior mind.

But while poets continue
To blow each other apart like dynamite
I want to write!
I want to change lives.
I want to touch somebody deep down inside!

I want to give the homeless mother new reasons to cope.
Let mine be the voice that encourages
That child born addicted to dope!
I want to write the words
That made me hold on while sickle cell found new
And improved ways to rip through my bones.
A fever that wouldn't check, swollen joints,
Inadequate insurance,
So doctors weren't trying to hear me moan.
I want to give that HIV positive child
New reasons to hold on.
I want to write the words that makes racists
Look upon themselves with scorn..
Shine light on date rape in college dorms.
Let me reach that neglected child
Who thought he was better off dead.
Let me write the words that needs to be said.
I want to write from that deep dark dirty disgusting place
That little girls retreat to when daddy
Secretly climbs in their bed!

Let my words regenerate, rejuvenate and revitalize,
Restore hope, restore health and breathe new life.
Let me write the words
To bring about an exemption from hostilities,
Give rebirth to liberty and tranquility,
Civility and chivalry.
That old fashion courtesy,
That keyboard harmony,
That long last gallantry.

From this stage I want to scream
The words that the world refuses to hear,
The so-called, *Unpopular Truth.*
Rip open my chest cavity
And share with you the scars of my youth.
Unveil this mask and show you the real face of child abuse!

Let me write the words
That causes the unproductive to produce!
Cultivate the uncultivated, and polish the rude.
Cause the unaccomplished
To implement, terminate, execute, dispatch and conclude.
Make the most hard-core Jamaican stand back and say,
"Gwaaan, my youth!"

If words can heal, then let me write the words
To remove hatred from at least one face.
Forget Black and White,
I want to write the poem that heals
And uplift the entire human race.
Take the junkie to that higher place,
Transcend time, energy and space.
But I refuse to be another poet
Who spits arrogance in your face!
So while others have egos to build
And inferiority complexes to fight,
Until the day I die,
I'VE GOT POEMS TO WRITE!

My Past (intro)

Love has evaded me
Escaped me,
Now this loneliness plagues me.
When I was younger, with love I was never concerned.
The only thing that was important was my ability to
maintain my groove,
I had that boxer's philosophy,
"Stick and move, stick and move!"
Don't get the emotions involved,
Keep the heart tucked away, buried deep within the soul,
My only prerequisite, a pulse and a hole,
No doubt I was cold.
Women in retrospect that I should've made my wife,
I found ingenious ways to sweep them out of my life.
Their tears flowed willingly,
As my illogical actions drove them insane,
And it seems that somewhere in my psyche,
I've cross-reference love and pain.

Came from a childhood where love was never expressed,
My parents stayed stressed, vexed.
At best they tolerated each other,
And the kids were a financial bother
I felt like I survived an abortion.
Or committed some deadly sin,
And family didn't seem like something
That "The Peoples Poet" needed to be in.
Sickle cell kept playing games with me,
Over and over again.

It would bring me to deaths door,
But wouldn't completely drag me in.
It would show me all the splendor of death.
The great escape
And I prayed it would take me in.
Instead it returned me to the dysfunctional family which
I was forced to live in.

In my teenage years I overheard my mom saying,
"There is no such thing as a good man!"
And with glee, my twenty-year-old sister agreed.
It was there I made the decision,
That I'll be damned if one of these floozie use me
Abuse and refuse me,
As long as I live I'm a do me!

By the time I got on the dating scene,
My heart was encased in steel walls.
Gave whatever compliment and conversation they needed.
In short I would talk my way to the drawz.
Entered loving relationships, thinking all problems solved,
Only problem is, my emotions would never get involved.
I've walked away from women who were perfect for me,
Left them pondering,
"What went wrong?"
"I can't even believe this!"
But, how could a grown man tell a woman
That his childhood broke him?
And at twenty-two he was still picking up the pieces.
Demons playing back voices inside my head,
The first two people I loved, return my love by saying,
"I wish you were dead"

So I walk away with sheltered emotions,
Trying not to feel guilty,
Fearing if I love you, you won't love me back,
And that would just kill me!
Baby I'm losing this battle against love fast,
Can't you see, **My Past Keep Kicking My Ass?**

My Past Keeps Kicking My Ass

They say that a cow never knows
The use of its tail until he loses it,
And a fool once he finds love,
Sure as hell abuses it!
Well, I be that fool, and I am that cow,
Because some way, somehow
I find "New and improved" ways
To destroy the love that we've built.
Before you know it, I'm off to the next, "Vic"
Leave you standing with the guilt.
I have you thinking that it was something you said
Or maybe even the things that you do,
When in fact, a fool like me
Doesn't deserve to be loved by you!

Coming from a past that I can't seem to get over,
And these Demons standing in the way
Won't allow us to get closer.
My Past Keep Kicking My Ass
And these demons won't let me go,
I keep reaching for your love and my past be like,
"Hell no!"
And I can't remember when this psychosis started,
But check the DNA of my soul
And you'll find fibers of a broken heart!

Baby, I'm coming from a past
Filled with just too many sorrows,
My demons saw you coming
And they snatched Cupid's arrows.

My Past Keep Kicking My Ass
And these demons won't let me be,
Won't let you get close to me.
I pray thee
Forgive me,
For changing the course of destiny,
Because I know that you are feeling me.
And I am on bending knees,
With God I plead,
Please release me
And let these demons set me free,
Because we were meant to be!

I've been a loner all my life!
Word! I wasn't looking for no wife,
Or someone to make me feel all warm inside,
Rob me of my foolish pride!
You said whenever you're alone
You can smell my cologne.
And I'm thinking, "Damn baby, how true!"
Because everything reminds me of you!
Or us two,
And the silly things that we do.
Across a crowded room you catch my stare,
And you know I'm thinking,
I wish these people would just disappear
I swear, I want you here, near.
But my demons are filled with fear!
They're protecting my heart,
About yours they don't care.
They'll do more to avoid pain
Than to gain any pleasure,
So they always find a way to bury my treasure!

As I take my hand and wipe the tears from your eyes,
Because I have no tissue,
I ask, "Why God?
Why did I have to come with so many issues?
Why must my past dictate my future?
This woman loves me but you insist that I lose her!"
Our attraction runs far more than the physical,
She moves me on levels far deeper than the spiritual.
She has eyes, eyes for no one but me,
And at first I thought it was the bald head,
The goatee, maybe even the poetry!
But it was on a deeper level that she was feeling me!

Her eyes have that divine honesty,
She possessed such modesty but subconsciously,
I don't think that I deserve you,
So I find new and improved ways to jerk you,
Unnerve you!
Determined not to let *YOU* and *I* become *WE*
But you find new and improved ways to forgive me,
Which leaves me feeling more and more unworthy!
So even though you are here
And I'm feeling you the most,
My past warns not to let you get close.
It questions your every move,
Measure your quality time by the ounce.
It shelters my emotions
So it wouldn't even matter if you decided to bounce!
And you asked, "How can I be so callous,
When deep down you know that I care?"
But I swear, the real question is my dear,
Can you who is motivated by love,
Reform me, who is motivated by fear?

My Past Keeps Kicking My Ass
And these demons won't let me go,
Saying, you're a friend now,
But sooner or later you'll be a foe.

Making general comparisons,
Showing me all there is to fear,
My past won't allow me to focus
On your beauty growing here.
And baby I have nothing, nothing but regrets,
Damn near three decades
And I still haven't learned how to love yet,
As I search the crevices of my mind,
Wondering why all my relationships
Seem like I'm doing time,
And it's only after I destroy the beauty
That I had with you,
Where I stop and think, "Oh God! Déjà vu"

I'm tired, tired of all this hurting,
Perfect relationship, six months later it ain't working!
Then you tell me that love conquers all,
But it was the abuse of love that built these walls,
So no longer do I give my all.
Cause when you step, I have nothing left.
Forget what you've been told,
Emotionally I'm cold
There are only burnt bridges to my soul.
So even though you feel so right
And you make me feel so whole,
To get you out of my life is the subconscious goal.
Yeah you make me feel complete,
When I'm with you
The world becomes an oyster at my feet.
But my past keeps looking for deceit
Telling me sooner or later you'll creep,
Sooner or later you'll trample my heart under your feet.
So in fear I retreat without being discreet,
And once again my life becomes bittersweet!

My Past Keeps Kicking My Ass,
And baby it ain't fair to you,

Wondering where we went wrong;
You ain't got a clue,
Because I keep feeding you
From a past menu
Residue of old rendezvous,
That I can't seem to undo.
And there's only so much that you can deal with,
It's just a matter of time before you get tired
Of the bull!
You gave me love and I abused it,
But this destiny, baby I didn't choose it.
I hope you find the courage to forgive me,
I swear, my intentions were not to hurt thee.
My actions I cannot condone,
And it seems like I'm destined to be alone.
As you walked through the door,
You told me that my relationships will never last,
Until I find a way
TO KICK MY PAST IN THE ASS!

I'm Falling For You

I've been to 2 continents,
3 countries
4 islands
34 different states.
Yet when I look at you,
I can't recall every seeing a more beautiful face.
Your eyes seems brighter,
Your smile whiter and I cherish your embrace.
Damn baby it seem like I'm falling
Cupid is calling.
This feeling is new,
Girl you gonna mess around
And make me fall in love with you.
I'm overcome by you
Don't know what to do,
Cause it feels like I'm falling...I'm falling in love.

I never believed in true love
Or true beauty until I laid eyes on you.
In your baby blue tennis shoe by Fubu
Mini skirt from Saks Fifth Avenue,
Hairdo that was brand spanking new.
Your beauty floored me like ninjitsu.
If only for a minute, I wanted you to be
The Pokemon master and I could be Pikachu,
So my Thunder shock could spark
Dormant desires in you,
And I could be in your pocket forever
Like the Internal Revenue.
Service whatever needs to be serviced.
Just let me do what I do.
Because your smile left a residue
That hit like Kung Fu,
Girl you knocked me off my feet!
The very thought of you

Makes my heart skip two or three beats,
Your lips were God's first masterpiece.
You are the girl that I idolize when I fantasize,
A little more than a mouthful
Was her perfect breast size.
Longing to excavate the treasures
Between her thighs
And it seems like I'm falling,
Girl stop! before I start loving you.

Regardless of what I did, consciously
Or unconsciously she was a part of that choice.
We just got off the phone
And I'm longing for her voice,
Oh God I'm falling!
We would listen to, "Say yes" by the Whispers
As I kissed her, on the nape of her neck,
She confessed, "Oh baby that makes me wet."
Girl you gonna mess around and make me love you.
Can't you see I'm falling...falling fast,
Whatever voodoo she knew, the spell has been cast.

She was my forbidden fruit,
A passion that I feel compelled to mention,
Her nipples screamed for my attention.
With her breast I was thoroughly impressed.
So impressed that my heart retreated from society,
And devoted its life to
The worship of her chest!
Her golden stomach was the flatlands of Egypt,
Chiseled by a God who knew my weakness.
This was the only woman that for her
I wanted to be there!
Called out sick
Just to wash, shampoo and play in her hair.
She was the urgency lovers felt for each other,
A minute without her,
Became a thousand tomorrows.

Her mind was divine,
Our goals aligned.
I would school her on the middle passage,
Isis and Nefertiti,
She would murder me in chess and Jeopardy,
Then restore me with her poetry.
The taste of her lips gave me sanity
Her eyes gave me clarity.
You just don't understand her beauty!
I said, "Girl you gotta stop doing
The things that you do,
You gonna mess around
And make me love you!"

My passion was useless to deny,
Because it was impossible to conceal,
To hell with Holyfield, she was the real deal!
How else do you explain a poet lacking the words
To explain what he feels?
I have no expectations, no demands,
Just want to spend some time in her arms.
Baby your beauty is illogical, irrational,
Unreasoned and unwarranted,
There is no reason for you to be so attractive,
Your beauty is almost unfair,
Extraordinary, beyond compare,
I would give up my spot on
Who Wants To Be A Millionaire?
Just so for you, a meal I could prepare.
Woman you are gorgeous squared.

She once spent the night,
Slept in my T-shirt
That stopped shy of her hips,
Her lips, her tits, her nips.
Yes she was 115 lbs of bliss.
Five foot two sweetheart was thick,
Dripping with oil, her body was ridic!
Her nipples rose to meet me,

Lower lips expanded to greet me,
Her essence completed me.
She had a body heat that was indiscrete,
A treat fit for the honeymoon suite,
How you say, "Ahhh bon appetit"
Her sweetness was diabetic,
And all the waters of the Earth could not dilute it.

I gave praises to the powers that be,
Because I could see
That the Gods were bent on blessing me.
Lovemaking was intense,
Like a cyclone spiraling through trees,
Hurricane Andrew penetrating the Florida Keys.
The entire church catching the Holy Ghost
On the day of Jubilee,.
She was as rare as a short line in the DMV
Unbelievable like the GOP backing
A candidate endorsed by the NAACP.
Her love was more intense
Than murder in the first degree.
She was sweeter than all the fruits of Waikiki.
And it seems like that loving feeling
Has gotten a hold of me.

Sometimes I gotta pinch myself,
Close my eyes and count to ten.
Cause when I'm with you,
I swear to God that I'm in Heaven.

Heaven

Heaven is between the Black woman's thighs,
If you've heard differently, you've been digesting lies,
You haven't seen true beauty
Until you look into those big brown eyes.
Until you kiss those luscious lips,
Then my son you cannot testify!
Keep your Vogue magazine,
Your European platters can't tempt me,
Because even my enemies admit
That my woman be *Ironically Sexy.*
I leave them pissed
Because their women have that flat behind,
Agitated, because my woman is so goddamn fine.
Perturbed because the sun favors mine the most,
And in winter my Jaquetta don't look like no ghost!
Winter, summer, fall, regardless of the season
Sisters be fine for no good goddamn reason!

If Heaven is between the Black woman's thighs,
Then I am a sanctified saint,
For I have been to that promised land that made me
Give away all Earthly possessions and say,
"Forget it, the landlord can wait!"
I've been to that promised land
That gives new meaning to life.

Left me sitting on a rock in Tibet, pondering,
"How could OJ trade in his Black wife?"
Don't want no implants, give me the real McCoy,
Because until you've been with a Black woman,
You don't know the meaning of *Almond Joy!*
All you've had is a sugar substitute.
You've been deceived from the days of your youth!

But as for me
I live and die for my *Baby Ruth,*
Just to kiss and caress her *Butterfinger* all night long,
Right into the break of day,
Climb her caramel *Mounds* and discover her *Milky Way.*
I pledge allegiance to the Black woman for I am her man,
I would pay *100 Grand* just for a glimpse of her perfection!
Not for all the diamonds in the world,
The rubies and pearls,
I would never forfeit the sweetness of her *Whatchamacallit.*
The thing with the tight fit
The troubled soul repair kit,
The passion pit with a warmth that just won't quit,
The banana split that leaves me throwing fits
Even made Mike Tyson give away his championship.

The *Kit Kat* that feels like *Payday*
The passageway that's off-*Broadway*
The sweet reward on display under the negligee,
That makes everyday feels like Christmas,
Or better yet my birthday.
The utopia that I dream of when it's time to get *Nutrageous.*
The great motivator that make brothers courageous.
I would love to brag that,
"I'm strictly business when I'm all up in that good stuff."
But Lord knows I go coo coo for *Cocoa Puffs.*

Wrapped around my ebony chocolate like a *Twizzler,*
Have my *Twix* all up in her,
Her back arched and her body folds,
I felt her *Nestle Crunch* as she moved to the *Tootsie Roll.*

Lips encircled her *Mounds*, and our bodies gave off steam,
Few more thrust of the *Hershey Bar*
And I felt her cookie creamed!
As I double dipped in her chocolate chip,
Betwixt her hips
My fudge got hot
We were dripping with butterscotch.
She rocked my world,
As I worked her *Chocolate Swirl*,
Left me screaming, "You go girl!"

Heaven is between the Black woman's thighs,
And she's my only aphrodisiac,
If she was a crime, I would be a kleptomaniac,
If she was a sickness, I would be a hypochondriac,
Her fire burning with desire makes me a pyromaniac
Regardless of the circumstance, I take my coffee black.
She is that first ray of sunshine after a category 4 hurricane,
She's the word that Webster could not explain
The Demerol that eases my emotional pain,
The Queen that captures the King
In this mortal chess game.
Of the Black woman
I have no complaints!

She's the reason I maintain,
Have me screaming Jesus' name.
She calls me, "Captain Kirk"
When I'm navigating that uncharted terrain.
She works me like a slave in the barnyard,
Makes me cum so hard
That the dresser, mirror and headboard
Stood up and applaud.

Ebonicly speaking, the Black woman is phat,
Between her thighs is where Heaven be at.
That cinnamon eclair,
That forces men to stare,
That brownie with the coffee latte,

Jamaican beef patty.
That berry brown wheat toast,
West African gold coast,
Where I constantly overdose!

So if you have that Guinness stout stamina that won't die,
Combined with that cocoa butter brownie
That's the apple of your eye,
And she's willing to share
Her life time supply of pumpkin pie.
Allow you to sink in her fountain with your poetic pen,
Her caramel clutch releases all of your adrenaline,
As you become the patient and she becomes the RN.
Together you explode every now and then,
Making you want a white picket fence,
A dog and two children,
And the world seems like a better place to live in.
Then my son look no further,
You're in heaven!

Pictures

Activist and Artist pose for picture after radio show at WLIB (1190 A.M) From left to right: *Alton Maddox, Tehut-Nine, Kirk Nugent, and Rev. Al Sharpton*

Poet Kirk Nugent (on right) stand with the father of Amadou Diallo during police brutality rally on Broadway in NYC.

Pictures

Kirk Nugent performing at The Nuyorican Poets Cafe in NYC.

Dr. Leonard Jeffries (left) and **The People's Poet** (right)

About the author

Kirk Nugent

Title: 1999 Nuyorican Grand Slam Champion
Alias: The People's Poet
Home mic: The World

Hard hitting, poignant and thought provoking, this 1999 Nuyorican Poets Cafe Grand Slam Champion is a spoken word icon. Born and raised in Kingston, Jamaica, Kirk Nugent is affectionately known as, "The People's Poet."

Nugent has been performing poetry throughout the United States for three years. In 1999 he was featured in CBS "60 Minutes" television special covering slam poetry. The People's Poet has performed on college campuses all across the United States and Canada. Kirk has opened for the Queen Latifah Show and a host of Def Jam and B.E.T comics, as well as shared the stage with Reverend Al Sharpton and Attorney Alton Maddox. He was the Captain of the 1999 Nuyorican National Slam Team. He was also the coach of the 2000 Nuyorican National Team. Kirk is a visionary and definitely one of the hardest working poets in the U.S. He recently released his spoken word CD entitled, "The Return of The People's Poet." He is the founder and CEO of Ironic Revolutionary Wear, and Ironically Sexy clothing line.

For more information about this cutting edge poet, email him at Kirkdpoet@aol.com
or visit
WWW.IRONICWORLD.COM